C000098194

THE LITTLE BOOK OF
PRINCE

Published by OH!
20 Mortimer Street
London W1T 3JW

ISBN 978-1-78739-374-5

Compiled by: Malcolm Croft
Project Editor: Ross Hamilton
Design: Russell Knowles, Luana Gobbo
Production: Rachel Burgess

A CIP catalogue record for this book is available from the British Library

Printed in Dubai

10 9 8 7 6 5 4 3 2

Jacket cover photograph: Getty Images

THE LITTLE BOOK OF
PRINCE

WISDOM AND WONDER FROM THE
LOVESEXY SUPERSTAR

CONTENTS

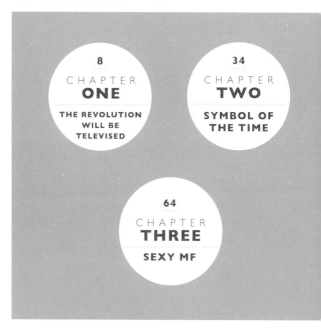

INTRODUCTION

Little did the world know on June 7, 1958, that the future Prince of rock and roll would be five feet two inches tall, sing in a register usually only enjoyed by puppies, and have a penchant for all things purple. Yes, Prince made sticking out like a sore thumb look sexy and cool without ever seeming like he was trying that hard.

In his tenure at the top of the pops, from his first self-produced record *For You* (1978) to his global monster album and film *Purple Rain* (1984) and beyond, Prince may have performed under a plethora of names, but Minnesota's favorite son was beloved for being just one thing: the bridge that united pop, funk, soul, dance, jazz and rock together in a way the world had never heard before. Or since.

Prince's early days growing up in a "black and white world" in Minnesota may have been as dysfunctional as those of many other 80s rock icons, but that's where any colorless clichés stop dead. As soon as Prince Rogers Nelson broke ground on his first record in 1978, the gloves came off and on squeezed the high heels and crushed velvet catsuits. You could not hold the man—or his music—back.

Dearly beloved, we gather together for this book to enjoy that thing called Prince's life. With his highness gone, all that is left of the man today is his timeless music. As he was never one for interviews, this collection of quotes and quips stands as a last will and testament of a musician who will long be revered as a one-of-a-kind, irreplaceable talent. The genuine article; the real deal: there will never be another quite like him. If music can be embodied by just one man, Prince be thy name. Enjoy!

CHAPTER

ONE

THE REVOLUTION
WILL BE TELEVISED

"

Everybody always stops talking or doing anything when I walk in! They say it's the artist who changes, but, I don't know, I really think it's everybody else.

2015

"

I play music. I make records. I make
movies. I don't do interviews.

1990

The most important thing is to be true to yourself, but I also like danger. That's what's missing from pop music today. There's no excitement or mystery.

1982

The key to longevity is to learn every aspect of music that you can.

2010

"

All people care about nowadays is getting paid, so they try to do just what the audience wants them to do. I'd rather give people what they need rather than just what they want.

"

1982

Like books and black lives, albums still matter.

2015

The record industry can be a wonderful system, if you want to go that route. After all, some people don't want the hassle of getting on the phone and talking to retailers about their own records; they want someone to do it for them. I'm just not one of those people.

1997

Each song writes itself. It's already perfect.

1997

I was brought up in a black and white world. I dig black and white; night and day, rich and poor, man and woman. I listen to all kinds of music and I want to be judged on the quality of my work, not on what I say, nor on what people claim I am, nor on the color of my skin.

1998

When I was rehearsing with Beyoncé for the Grammys, I sat her down at the piano and I helped her to learn just some simple scales and then tried to encourage her to learn the piano because there's a language that musicians know that's a little different than, say, just a singer.

2004

A lot of times I didn't know I was pushing the envelope until later. In today's climate you've got everybody thinking that that's a holy grail to do something explicit. And what happens is it's not explicit anymore because everybody's doing it.

2004

I can't help but be sexy. I mean, that's just what it is. You know, sex isn't so much what you say. It's how you say it and the way you sing, you know? It just comes out that way.

2004

I would ask people who want to call this record a comeback where they think I'm coming back from.

2004

When you show you can be successful as an independent artist, the umbilical cord is broken. Record contracts are a parent–child relationship. An advance is an allowance. **"**

2004

"

Sometimes I hear a melody in my head, and it seems like the first color in a painting. And then you can build the rest of the song with other added sounds. You just have to try to be with that first color, like a baby yearns to come to its parents. That's why creating music is really like giving birth.

1988

"

Music is like the universe: the sounds are like the planets, the air and the light fitting together.

1988

"

My bassist, Sonny T., can play a girl's measurements on his instrument and make you see them. I love the idea of visual sounds.

"

1988

When I wrestled with demons, I had moods when I couldn't figure something out and so I ran to vice to sort myself out, like women or too much drink, or working in order to avoid dealing with the problem.

1988

Attention to detail makes the difference between a good song and a great song. And I meticulously try to put the right sound in the right place, even sounds that you would only notice if I left them out.

1988

Prince Rogers Nelson is on my birth certificate. My father wanted me to be a star, so he named me Prince.

1997

"

Writers often use the word 'prolific' with me, but I don't think that's right. When you're committed to something like we are, when you spend the amount of time on something that we do, then you're bound to create a lot. This is what we do. This is our job.

"

2015

Everyone has their own experience. That's why we are here, to go through our experience, to learn, to go down those paths, and eventually you may have gone down so many paths and learned so much that you don't have to come back again.

1996

"

When I was younger, I had a massive ego. *Massive.* But that's not such a bad thing. Because at least you're aspiring to be something; you consider yourself great because you want to be great.

1996

"

When I became a symbol, all the writers were cracking funnies, but I was the one laughing. I knew I'd be here today, feeling as if each new album is my first.

2004

CHAPTER

TWO

SYMBOL
OF THE TIME

I didn't let fame rule me.

2004

You only get famous once. The audience you have is the audience you always have.

2004

"

Really, I'm normal. A little highly strung, maybe. But normal. But so much has been written about me and people never know what's right and what's wrong. I'd rather let them stay confused.

2004

"

Music is everything to me. I love making music. I am making music. Music is spirit, it's therapy. It makes me feel a certain way, and if played with conviction and soul, the same thing occurs in other people. **"**

2004

Prince is dead. They [Warner Bros. Records] killed him. I don't own Prince's music. If you don't own your masters, your master owns you.

1993

Musicians inherited this system, so that's how most musicians work, how we get the music to the people. But it used to be the tradition to have slaves on the plantation. Don't mean it's right!

1993

I'm no different to anyone. Yes, I have fame and wealth and talent, but I certainly don't consider myself any better than anyone who has no fame, wealth or talent. People fascinate me. Life fascinates me! And I'm no more fascinated by my own life than by anyone else's.

1996

I ran away from home when I was 12. I've changed address in Minneapolis 32 times, and there was a great deal of loneliness. But when I think about it, I know I'm here for a purpose, and I don't worry about it so much.

1981

"

I don't need no producer, I don't need no record company, no A&R man or anyone telling me what to do. I produce my own records in my own studio. Why do I need someone telling me what to do, and owning what I do?

"

1993

I don't let computers use me. It's more interesting to me to pick up a guitar and create a sound out of thin air. That's analog. We're analog creatures; we breathe air, we hear sound waves, we react to spirit and color. A computer's binary.

2011

I do feel like a punk, because no one believes in God anymore.

1996

If you put a loaf of bread on the table, it turns into medicine and to me that is incredible. The bread will eventually take care of itself. That's nature, that's the Truth.

1996

I know those paths of excess, drugs, sex and alcohol – all those experiences can be funky, they can be very funky, but they're just paths, a diversion, not the answer…

1996

I find freedom sexy. I find freedom so sexy I can't even explain it to you. You wake up every day and feel like you can do anything.

1996

"

I was constantly running from family to family. It was nice on one hand, because I always had a new family, but I didn't like being shuffled around. I was a bitter kid for a while, but I adjusted.

1984

"

Everything about my music is autobiographical.

1981

Dirty Mind really felt like me for once. When I brought it to the record company it shocked a lot of people. But they didn't ask me to go back and change anything, and I'm really grateful. I wasn't being deliberately provocative… I was being deliberately me.

1981

I hear things in my sleep; I walk around and go to the bathroom and try to brush my teeth and all of a sudden the toothbrush starts vibrating! That's a groove!

1985

"

People think I'm a crazy fool for writing 'slave' on my face. But if I can't do what I want to do, what am I? When you stop a man from dreaming, he becomes a slave. That's where I was.

1996

I'm not the Artist Formerly Known as Anything. Use my name.

1993

"

I'm not saying I'm better than anybody else. But I'll be sitting there at the Grammys, and U2 will beat you. And you say to yourself, 'Wait a minute. I can play that kind of music. But they can't do 'Housequake'.'

1990

You know when you buy someone's record and there's always an element missing? The voice is wrong or the drums are lame or something? On mine there's nothing missing.

1991

I make music because if I don't, I'd die. I record because it's in my blood. I hear sounds all the time. It's almost a curse: to know you can always make something new.

1991

"

I play a lot of styles. This is not arrogance; this is the truth. Sometimes I just stand in awe of what I do myself. I feel like a regular person, but I listen to *Emancipation* and wonder, 'Where did it come from?'.

"

1996

"

It's a blessing and a curse these days that I'm competing with my older music. And I don't know anybody who has to do that. They always play Beyoncé's latest track. But I go on *Oprah* and they want me to play what *they* remember.

"

2014

I think when one discovers himself he discovers God. Or maybe it's the other way around.

1985

Music was put on earth to enlighten and empower us and feel closer to our center.

1998

There's an incredible peace in my life now and I'm trying to share it with people.

2010

CHAPTER

THREE

SEXY MF

Larry King asked me once, 'Didn't you need a record company to make it?'. But that has nothing to do with it. You don't need a record company to turn you into anything. I had autonomous control from the very beginning.

2015

You know how easy it would have been to just put it in a different key? That would have shut everybody up who said the album wasn't half as powerful! I don't want to make an album like the earlier ones, you dig?

1985

I don't want to be the CEO of anything. No titles. The minute you've accepted a title you're a slave to it. You're no longer free. The more people you allow to come between you and your music, the further it moves away from you. This isn't your business, it's your life.

1998

There's nothing a critic can tell me that I can learn from. If they were musicians, maybe. But I hate reading about what some guy sitting at a desk thinks about me.

1990

The more I think about it, the more music is all just based on colors and sounds. Miles Davis wasn't thinking in terms of bridging. People wanted to play with him because they knew he wasn't going to bow to any rules. A strong spirit transcends rules.

2000

More than anything else, I try not to repeat myself. It's the hardest thing in the world to do — there's only so many notes one human being can muster.

1985

When a person does get a hit, they try to do it again the same way. I don't think I've ever done that. I think that's the problem with the music industry today.

1985

People describe me as a loving tyrant. I'm probably the hardest band leader to work for, but I do it for love.

2011

Purple Rain was 100 shows, and around the 75th, I went crazy.

2011

The challenge is to outdo what I've done in the past. I play each show as if it's the last one.

2011

"

I love growing older. The older I get the closer I am to where I'm going, which is a better place. We all have a purpose within us. We are put here for a reason. My talent is God-given, but the music is made by me. I make the choices that make the music.

"

1996

"

If I need psychological evaluation,
I'll do it myself.

2011

"

The sooner this thing called fame goes away, the better. We got people who don't need to be famous.

2011

For me, fame happened very fast. One time, I had some old clothes on because I was going to help a friend move house and some girls came by and one went: 'Oh my god, Prince!' And the other girl pulled a face and said, 'That ain't Prince.' I didn't come out of the house raggedy after that.

2011

"

Michael Jackson and I both came along at a time when there was nothing. MTV didn't have anyone who was visual. Bowie, maybe. A lot of people made great records but dressed like they were going to the supermarket.

"

2011

How many people have substance and how many are just putting on crazy clothes?

2011

Well, I don't think it. I know it.

Prince, when asked "Do you think you're good?", 2011

Anyone who was around back then knew what was happening. When they were sleeping, I was jamming. I was working. When they woke up, I had another groove. I'm as insane that way now as I was back then.

1990

Half the things people were writing about me were true.

1990

Cool means being able to hang with yourself. All you have to ask yourself is: 'Is there anybody I'm afraid of? Is there anybody who if I walked into a room and saw, I'd get nervous?' If not, then you're cool.

1990

You can always renegotiate a record contract. You just go in and say, 'You know, I think my next project will be a Country & Western album.'

1990

I am what I am. I feel if I can please myself musically, then I can please others, too.

1990

Some might not get it. But people also said *Purple Rain* was unreleasable. And now I drive to work each morning to my own big studio.

1990

I'm not trying to be this great visionary wizard. Perfection is in everyone. It's not just something that I have the keys to. Nobody's perfect, but they can be. We may never reach that, but it's better to strive than not.

1985

"

You've got to understand that there's only so much you can do on an electric guitar. There are only so many sounds a guitar can make. Lord knows I've tried to make a guitar sound like something new to myself.

1985

"

Today, people don't write songs; they're a lot of sounds, a lot of repetition. That happened when producers took over, and that's why there's no more live acts. There's no box office anymore. The producers took over, and now nobody wants to see these bands.

1985

Kids save a lot of money for a long time to buy tickets, and I like to give them what they want. When I was a kid, I didn't want to go hear James Brown play something I never heard before. I wanted to hear him play something I knew, so I could dance.

1990

Mick Jagger said he hoped he wouldn't be singing 'Satisfaction' at thirty, and he's still singing it. Pete Townshend wrote, 'Hope I die before I get old.' Well, now he is old, and I do hope he's happy to be around. I don't want to say anything that can be held against me later!

1990

When I pray to God, I say, 'It's your call – when it's time to go, it's time to go. But as long as you're going to leave me here, then I'm going to cause much ruckus!'

1990

The first line in that song is 'Your butt is mine.' Now, I was saying to Michael, 'Who's gonna sing that to whom? 'Cause you sure ain't singin' that to me! And I sure ain't singin' that to you. Right there, we got a problem.'

1997

"

The internet's like MTV. At one time MTV was hip and suddenly it became outdated. Anyway, all these computers and digital gadgets are no good. They just fill your head with numbers and that can't be good for you.

2013

"

Record contracts are just like – I'm gonna say the word – slavery. I would tell any young artist… don't sign.

1996

The music I make a lot of the time
is reflective of the life I am leading.

1997

When you wake up, each day looks the same, so each day should be a new beginning. I don't have an expiration date.

2010

Listen to *Emancipation* and you will hear what a free man sounds like.

1996

You give a man a million dollars, he's a millionaire. But there is still higher to go, isn't there? You give someone like me all he's ever wanted, which is a recording studio, and that's it, right? There is nothing else for me to get, nothing else to buy.

1996

"

I hope to see the day that all men are free and can make things as free men, whether it's a building, a car or a neighborhood. How would our neighborhoods be? What would we do in a perfect world where we are completely free?

"

1996

I play a diverse range of styles, I
always have, and it's really hard to
do everything that you are feeling
on one album of nine songs. I just
do too much. **"**

1996

CHAPTER

FOUR

PURPLE REIGN

The record business is like *The Matrix*. All the levels keep dissolving until you can't see what's behind anything. I'm not against the record industry. Their system is perfect. It benefits the people who it was designed to benefit: the owners.

1999

I had to get out of the recording industry, and once I did, that changed my perspective on everything. It's like climbing a mountain: the higher you get, the more you can see. I had to get out of the system to see it.

1999

It's a good and a bad thing that I live here. It's bad in the sense that I can't be a primo 'rock star.' I can't go to the parties and be at all the awards shows. But I like it here. It's really mellow.

On Paisley Park, 1985

I don't mind my picture being taken if it's done in a proper fashion. It's very easy to say, 'Prince, may I take your picture?' I don't know why people can't be more humane about a lot of things they do.

1985

I was never rich, so I have very little regard for money now. I only respect it inasmuch as it can feed somebody. I give a lot of it away. Money is best spent on someone who needs it. That's all I'm going to say. I don't like to make a big deal about it.

1985

The reason I didn't use other musicians on my records a lot of the time had to do with the hours that I worked. I swear to God it's not out of boldness when I say this, but there's not a person around who can stay awake as long as I can. Music is what keeps me awake.

1985

"

I don't look for whether something's cool or not. If I do something that I think belongs to someone else or sounds like someone else, I do something else.

1985

"

I think it is very hard for a band to make it in Minneapolis, even if they're good. Mainly because there aren't any big record companies or studios in this state. I really feel that if we would have lived in Los Angeles or New York or some other big city, we would have made it big by now.

1976

Record companies are run by men who think they run America. They think they're the smartest but they're not. They don't know what's going on in my mind.

1995

Once the internet is a reality the music business is finished. There won't be any need for record companies. If I can send you my music direct, what's the point of having a music business?

1995

As the millennium approaches, we all must look inward and speak the truth. I had a boss, and I didn't like it. No more than you like it. I feel free now that there's no daddy around to spank me. It's time for us to stand up for what we believe in.

1998

You don't know how much it hurts not owning your own material. When a record company goes ahead and does something with a song you wrote… it can make you angry for a week.

1998

> I follow what God tells me to do. He said, 'Change your name,' and I changed my name to a symbol ready for internet use before I knew anything about the internet.

1999

I've always dressed the way I've wanted to and if it goes with the music, it's only because the music is part of me and so is the way I dress. I don't try to do anything to shock people or to make money — that would make me a hooker.

1981

"

Carlos Santana. Jimi Hendrix. James Brown, of course. They all influenced me. On piano, I was influenced by my father, who was influenced by Duke Ellington and Thelonious Monk. I like to say I took from the best.

"

1999

People's perception of me changed after *Purple Rain*, and it pigeonholed me. I saw kids coming to concerts who screamed just because that's where the audience screamed in the movie. That's why I did *Around the World in a Day*, to totally change that. I wanted not to be pigeonholed.

1999

I know that people want to talk about the past. We're not at *Purple Rain* anymore. We don't look like that, we don't dress like that, we're different people now. If you talk about that, the next thing you know, people start writing things like the Revolution is going to reunite!

1999

Record companies expect their artists to lose their voice, their hair and their energy. I'm not doing any of that.

1999

"

Malcolm X thinks differently than Malcolm Little [his birth name]. When you're trying to change, you have to divorce yourself from the past.

"

1999

I skipped school a lot, but I graduated early; dismissal was my favorite time of day. I believe in teachers, but not for me. Anything creative I don't think can be taught, otherwise you get somebody else's style; it's not yours, it's theirs.

1979

I'm a writer. Stephen King is a writer. Can I take a page out of his book and call it Prince's *Shining*? Can I take a scene out of a movie and call it my own? They say the law helps the writers. I don't need help; I don't need your money. Let us steward our own music.

2004

It took me four albums to get on the cover of *Rolling Stone*. Now it takes new artists only one. There should be rules for that kind of thing!

2004

Paisley Park is the place one should find in oneself, where one can go when one is alone.

1985

All these hip-hop artists today, the first thing they do is start their own label and lock their business down — I had a lot to do with that.

2004

I saw myself as an instrumentalist who started singing out of necessity. To me, my voice is just like one of the instruments I play. It's just one thing I do.

1978

We were wined and dined by a lot of companies, but when everybody else was talking gifts and bonuses, the people at Warner Brothers were actually listening to the demo.

1978

I like the ones with nice personalities.

On women, 1979

By the time I was a sophomore, school had gotten to be a real drag. I was getting further and further into making music. The more I found myself entertaining at local gigs during the night, the more I hated the thought of going to school in the morning.

1978

"

I'm not entangled in a bunch of lawsuits and a web that I can't get out of. I can hold my head up... a happily married man who has his head in order. There isn't a bunch of scandal in my life.

"

2004

I always knew I had a relationship with God. But I wasn't sure God had a relationship with me.

2004

No one can come and claim
ownership of my work. I am the
creator of it, and it lives within me.

2004

"

I was seventeen, a graduate, and frustrated. I felt that I had to keep going after the music but didn't know how long I'd be able to do it and eat too. I did know that I wanted something more than just a nine-to-five.

"

1978

"

Embarrassed? I don't know that word. Have you seen my outfits?

2004

"

What it all boils down to means nothing except love. As long as I got that, I don't need money. If I went broke, it wouldn't faze me. Love and music. As long as I got that, everything's cool. Everything.

1979

"

Once you learn piano, everything else falls into place.

1981

"

I'm only a conductor of whatever electricity comes from the world, or wherever we all come from. To me the ultimate responsibility is the hardest one – the responsibility to be true to myself.

1981

"

It's all just part of the dream factory. If it happens, it happens. It's best not to even worry about that, 'cause if you strive for it and don't get it, you'll be disappointed and feel like a failure.

"

1979

If it wasn't against the law, I wouldn't wear anything.

1981

"

I find it a lot easier to sing swear words than to say them and when I first had a girl, I found it really hard to tell my mother but, Lord knows, I didn't feel embarrassed while I was doing it to her.

"

1981

I don't want to just be doing what's expected of me. I just want to live... until it's time to die...

1981

FIVE

PARTYMAN

People call me a prodigy. I don't even know what the word really means. I'm just a person.

1981

I remember I had this song called 'Machine' that was about this girl that reminded me of a machine. It was very explicit about her, er, parts. People seemed to find it very hard to take.

1981

I only write from experience. I don't plan to shock people. I write about things I guess people are afraid to talk about.

1981

I think my father was kind of lashing out at my mother when he named me Prince.

1980

"

My dad left home for the first time and left his piano. He never let anyone play it before. So I taught myself songs from the television – *Batman, Man from U.N.C.L.E.* I learned to play them by ear.
"

1981

When the charts and awards are coming in your favor, they are the greatest thing in the world. When they are not working in your favor, they are absolutely meaningless.

1981

My dad was in a jazz band, and I went to watch one of his gigs when I was about five. I was supposed to stay in the car, but I snuck out and went into the bar. He was up on stage and it was amazing. I remembered thinking, 'These people think my dad is great.' I wanted to be part of that.

1981

I'm not saying I'm better than anybody else, but I don't feel like there are a lot of people out there telling the truth in their music.

1981

I get $7 an album now. If I sell 100,000 albums — which they consider a failure — I've got $700,000 in the bank. That's cool. I've got the money in the bank. I'm holding the puppies, you dig?

1998

I want to make sure I'm dealing with the guy who hands you the money rather than the guy that hands you the bill, you know what I'm sayin'?

1998

"

I always compare songwriting to a girl walking in the door. You don't know what she's going to look like, but all of a sudden she's there.

1981

When I first got started in music, I was attracted by the same things that attract most people to this business. I wanted to impress my friends and I wanted to make money. For a while, I just did it as a hobby. Then it turned into a job and a way to eat. Now I look on it as art.

1981

"

I realized after *Dirty Mind* that I can get away with anything I want to get away with. All I have to do is be true to myself. I can make the records I want to make and still be OK. I feel free.

"

1981

You can say a bad word over and over again and sooner or later it won't be bad anymore if everybody starts doing it.

1983

I think I change constantly, because I can hear the music changing. The other day I put my first three albums on and listened to the difference. And I know why I don't sound like that any more. Because things that made sense to me and things that I liked then I don't like anymore.

1983

"

I think *Purple Rain* is the most avant–garde thing I've ever done. Just look at the singles 'When Doves Cry' and 'Let's Go Crazy.' Most artists won't try a groove like that.

"

1986

"

In the '60s, when everybody tried to be different, you had War and Santana, and Hendrix, and Sly, and James Brown, and they were all uniquely different. Now, everyone just jumps on what they think are the hottest sounds.

"

1986

I'm not saying that I'm great or anything like that; I'm just saying that I'm an alternative. I'm something else. And I long to hear something else from everybody. There are a lot of talented people out there. I just don't think they go far enough.

1986

I'm very stubborn, real bull-headed. If I want something, I really fight for it, if I really believe in it. The first album *For You*, I really believed that I should produce it. The people in power tried to put me in with what was the happening sound, the few cats on top. I wanted to get away from that.

1986

Money runs out, but music appreciates like real estate.

1999

“

I just want to be all that I can be.

1994

”

If people think I'm insane, fine. I want people to think I'm insane. But I'm in control. I'm not playing anyone else's game. I don't care if people say I'm mad. It don't matter.

1995

I have free will, and I'm ecstatic. There is no ceiling now – no limits. I can see the sky.

1999

You don't.

,,

Prince, when asked
"So, how do you pronounce it?"
about his Love Symbol moniker, 1994

"

A woman in climax.

"

**Prince, when asked,
"What is your idea of the ultimate
guitar tone?", 1994**

Back when I was coming up, I didn't dress like anybody, I didn't look like anybody, I didn't sound like anybody. I still try to do that. Why do what everybody else is doing?

2004

"

I don't see myself as an icon. I don't see that. I didn't put myself on a pedestal. If I'm on a pedestal it's because other people have put me there.

1995

"

After I'm free from Warner Bros., it'll either be very quiet or very exciting. But it won't be in the middle. It'll be extreme. Life, I mean. It'll all be extreme.

1996

"

I worry about that. I worry whether people are going to be ready for what I do.

1996

I really feel a need to school a new generation of musicians. Technology is cool, but you've got to use it as opposed to letting it use you.

2004

Music, for me, doesn't come on a schedule. I don't know when it's going to come, and when it does, I want it out.

1996

• 178

My name is the eye of me. It doesn't have a sound. It looks beautiful and makes me feel beautiful. Prince had too much baggage.

1996

There's always been a dichotomy in my music: I'm searching for a higher plane, but I want the most out of being on earth.

1996

Not to sound cosmic, but I've made plans for the next 3,000 years. Before, it was only three days at a time.

1996

"

I've gone several places in the world. And when I get back over that green and all those lakes, I feel peace. I think God puts you where you live for a reason, and I'll live in Minneapolis for the rest of my life.

1996

I never really needed approval for what it is that I do. I love that I'm appreciated and I love the respect that I get. But accolades and awards – you know it's all still big business.

2004

"

I'm a pretty open book. People who know my music I would say know me.

2004

"

I make a lot of money on the road. I make $300,000 a night. You add that up and you can see why people want to put a rope around an artist. And sales of music is not as important as giving people a night they're going to remember. I'd just as well give the music away.

1998

"

I do my music to excess. Music, music, music — it's like a curse that way. It can be a curse. It's been like that since I was seven years old and my father left for the last time. That's a lot to do with it. My sister used food and I used music.

"

1998

I had planned to do nothing in 1999 except reflect. I needed time off from the industry. Everyone said, 'But this is your year!' I stopped, I broke the pattern, I went away and didn't talk to anybody.

1999

66

Bowie and Madonna, even if it wasn't good, we still talk about them because it was something new. That's a beautiful word.

2004

99

There weren't a lot of artists who were free to say what they wanted to on records. And they were put into molds. The freedom that I had came from a long, hard fight of trying to get them to understand that I wanted to be different. **"**

2004

"

Life is a symphony, and we are all musicians. You are either in harmony or not. **"**

2000

I won't speculate on where the music came from. I look back in awe and reverence. It's made me become courageous.

1988

My goal is to excite and to provoke
on every level.

1981